FROM RAGS TO RICHES
NORTH COUNTRY RAG RUGS

THE BEAMISH COLLECTIONS

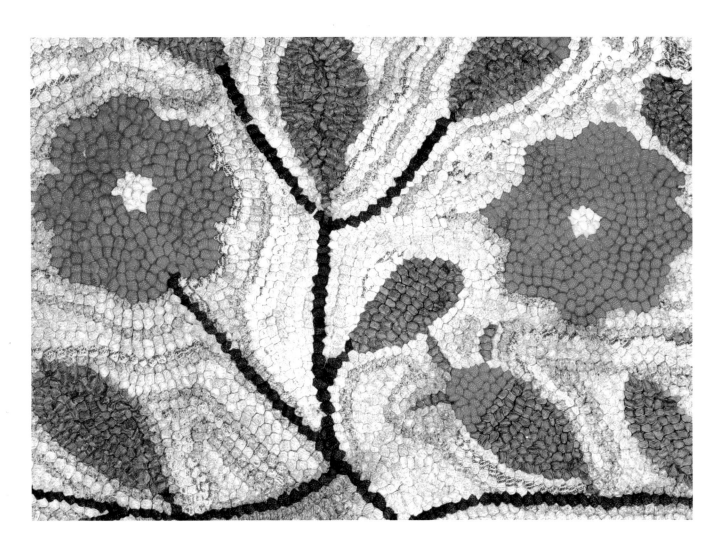

Rosemary E Allan

First published in 2007 by

Beamish,
The North of England Open Air
Museum

Beamish Museum Co.
Durham, DH9 ORG

Photography by
Rosemary E. Allan,
Justin Battong, Paul Castrey,
Duncan Davis, Julian Harrop,
David Lawson and Jim Lawson.

Design by
Ian Brown Design Ltd.

Printed in England by Elanders

British Library Cataloguing in
Publication Data.

A catalogue record for this book is
available from the British Library.

ISBN 0-905054-12-1

CONTENTS

FROM
RAGS TO RICHES
NORTH COUNTRY RAG RUGS

Hooky mat made on a pre stamped hessian, produced as design 'Alexandra' by the Newcastle Wool Co., Ltd. The rose and leaves, linked by the brown chain, are set on an imaginative background hooked in waving lines in complementary colours. The mat was made in Northumberland, and probably dates to the 1950s or later.

(2006-54)
1830 x 1120mm.

PREFACE

RAG RUGS OR RAG MATS, as they are sometimes called, are hard wearing rugs made from cuttings of material. The words 'rug' and 'mat' are synonymous, the term 'rug' being used in many parts of the British Isles as well as in the USA, though in the North of England, and in Nova Scotia, the preferred term is 'mat, and that is how they are referred to here.

These mats were very popular, especially in the mining villages and rural cottages of the North, where they were made, surviving examples dating from the mid 1800s to the 1960s. Rag mat making involved every member of the family and was an important part of family life, within the community. It is now appreciated as an important Folk Art survival.

The mat was being made in the space between the bed and the table. The large kitchen gave scope for many things to be carried on simultaneously. Mother could bake, father could bath, a meal could be going forward, and over in the corner, just by the bed, space could be used for the exercise of the pit-woman's craft — mat-making or quilting. A long stretch of canvas, ingeniously pleated to frames, which could be widened or narrowed by sliding laths or pins, the whole rested lightly on some rough support, such as chair, table, or even bed. Plonk, plonk, went the "progger" as Mary and Jinny pricked the hole, which was deftly filled by short pieces of dyed cloth. The workers' fingers, the drive of the pricker or "progger", and the working of the "clippings" into the canvas was a quick, continuous process, which made one whole. A little more staccato than tapestry- weaving, but deftness was the mark of it. All according to pattern desired, which was marked on the matting. And it was the Ross's own pattern. You didn't get it out of the Ladies' Own or send to London for some special design. This pattern was a family affair. Well, another family might have been let into the secret — but there was still pride in its scarcity and originality. Red, blue, greens, soft browns, all done in lines and curves with rough stuff, from old clothes, sometimes pit-clothes, washed, dyed and cut exact lengths by patient fingers. Yet the pattern would be as perfect as the pencilling of a trained artist. Indeed, these women were unconscious artists, product of generations of the craft, making soothing pictures out of waste odds and ends, and making them in odds and ends of time.'

...SO WROTE JACK LAWSON in 1934 in his novel **Under the Wheels**, which was based on his own life's experience of working in the coalmines of County Durham.

A rare photograph of a cottage interior, taken from an original glass plate, discovered on a tip at Consett. The photo, which is labelled 1892 Miners' Strike, depicts a typical domestic scene, with ladies hard at work at the mat frame, making a proggy mat, whilst the men folk have a game of dominoes and a glass of beer. The kitchen range can be seen in the background, together with some wonderful floral wallpaper. (73962)

Born, 16th October 1881, the son of a sailor / miner, who was almost illiterate, Jack began work in the mine at the age of twelve. The Durham Miners' Strike of 1892 had a significant impact on his family, and Jack, determined to improve himself as well as to help his fellow pitmen, became a committed trade unionist, working tirelessly to improve wages and conditions in the pits. Elected Member of Parliament for Chester le Street in 1919, he became Secretary of State for War in 1945, and was made Baron Lawson of Beamish in 1950.

Jack's novel portrays a scene typical of many a mining family in the North East of England, between the years 1850 and 1950. The making of rag mats was not only an everyday craft to be found in the industrial urban areas as well as in the rural countryside, it was also an important part of the social fabric of people's lives within these communities.

First and foremost, the craft was carried on from necessity,

originally in poorer households, which could not afford to purchase machine made floor coverings. In the early 19th century, older rural and industrial cottages had beaten earth floors. Many later working class homes and particularly miners' houses had stone flagged floors or were laid with firebricks, known as "quarrels" or "quarls". These floors tended to wear unevenly and would not have been suitable for carpets.

There had always been a tradition of decorating stone flags outside and inside the house, with sand or chalked patterns. In Cumberland "rudd", a soft red sandstone, was sold in bags in the local markets, and in other areas, "donkey stone", a manufactured product, was also used to create these designs. The making of rag mats was a logical progression, from this early decoration, as they provided not only comfort and colour, but also kept rooms cosy and took away the chill of stone floors. Sometimes, when a new mat was made, it took pride of place as a bed covering.

HISTORY OF THE CRAFT

The origins of rag mat making are extremely obscure. It has been suggested that the craft came from Europe, most likely Scandinavia, to Britain and to Scotland in particular, around the late 1400s, and that it arrived in the North of England around late Tudor times, lasting for several centuries. We cannot, however, be sure of its exact origins, as many of the accounts that have been written are conjecture.

Made to commemorate the Diamond Jubilee of Queen Victoria in 1897, this proggy mat, made in wools and tweeds, was rescued from a junk shop in Carlisle. The colours employed are subdued and represent typical clothing fabrics of the time. (1987-58) 1790 x 1005mm.

WILLIAM WINTHROP KENT, the American architect, author and authority on American Hooked Rugs, corresponded with a Miss Ann Macbeth of Hartsop, Patterdale, near Penrith in Cumberland in 1927. Ann Macbeth was a writer and had been teacher of handicrafts at the Glasgow School of Art, from 1908 until 1920. In her correspondence with Mr. Kent, she examines the designs on the carved furniture of Westmorland and Cumberland, looking at Bride wains and three and four tiered oak cupboards, comparing the scrolls and curves with the designs on mats. She saw no reason to discredit the theory, that these designs had been introduced by Scandinavian settlers. Whilst it is true that names of people, natural features and old household words, in parts of the North of England are strongly Scandinavian in origin, we cannot necessarily make a direct connection. The fashion in Scandinavia of covering the floors with rushes and making them into woven mats persisted in some Westmorland villages. In Norway, a technique of hooking loops through a base fabric was developed in place of skin rugs and these were often used on beds.

The Shetland islands, (owned by Norway until the 15th century), may have provided a link between the countries' cultures, as there was a strong rag mat making tradition on the islands, where these mats were required by each bride for her dowry, and this custom survived until the early years of the 20th century. A trade of itinerant rag mat makers developed, travelling from one island to the next, producing mats in exchange for their keep.

It would seem that the craft, as a European tradition, was taken to the eastern seaboard of America and Canada, by settlers from England and Scotland. Here mat hooking flourished and reached new heights of artistic creation. Early rag mats would be made on a linen backing, but from the 1830s, England began to import jute from India. After 1850, jute woven into hessian became readily available throughout both Europe and America. A number of firms on both sides of the Atlantic produced pictorial and floral designs, stencilled onto hessian, by mail order.

Sadly there is little or nor literature in England about rag mats. These were not the heirlooms to be listed in inventories or diaries and few accounts mention them. It is known that the craft was never widely developed and it was always regarded more as a cottage industry, and never as a fashionable handicraft. Jane Austen's **Emma** is recorded as saying 'If I give up music, I shall take to carpet work'.

Although the making of rag mats was an essential part of life in working class homes in the North, and in many other parts of the country, it was never considered respectable enough to be included in the many needlework magazines of the Victorian period. Very few photographs survive illustrating the craft and all we have

to go on is the physical evidence provided by the mats themselves. Older examples are few and far between. When a mat was completely worn out, it was thrown out.

In his book **The Hooked Rug** of 1930, Kent states of the craft, that *'the past neglect of it is strange in a land which has concerned itself wonderfully with the arts and crafts of other countries. Even the superb South Kensington Museum had not a specimen in 1922.'* They have since remedied this with the acquisition of a hooked rug designed and made, 1930-1935, by Rhoda Dawson, for the Grenfell Mission, in Labrador and Newfoundland. The Mission was founded in 1892 by an English doctor, Wilfred Grenfell, to support the welfare of the poor fishing communities and to serve the British immigrant community in the coastal villages. The craft of rug making was developed into a successful industry, many rugs being sold in America and even finding their way to Britain.

The Second World War brought about a renewed need to recycle and "make do and mend". Everything was used from lisle stockings to old blankets and parachute silk! The making of rag mats in the North of England, an area affected badly by the depression, continued well into the 1950s, and later. There was a gradual transition from the use of rags to wool thrums, which were readily available

Old lady, sitting at the matting frame, which is typically propped up on the kitchen table. Note the balls of clippings ready to go into the mat. The photograph was taken for an article in the Durham Advertiser newspaper. (22,416)

from northern carpet factories. The pre stamped hessians, specially designed for rag mats, which were sold from drapery stores, wool shops and the Co-op Stores, were also available in canvas, suitable for use with wool thrums. The craft imperceptively changed from being an occupation of necessity, to being a leisure pastime.

By the 1960s, it began to be recognised and appreciated, much more as an art form. Winifred and Ben Nicholson, the artists, working at Banks Head, Lanercost, Cumberland, had, since the 1920s, been inspired by the work of the older traditional mat makers, and working with their next-door neighbour, Margaret Warwick, a farmer's wife, went on to design their own mats. Their son Jake's textile company, Foursquare Designs, produced and sold well over a hundred mats, many designed by Winifred, in the 1970s. The designs were much influenced by local surroundings and often depicted a favourite cat, dog, sheep, cow or other pictorial scene.

In the 1980s, artists, Audrey and Denis Barker, formed the "Barkers of Lanercost", and produced some fine artistic designs for mats, which were made by a group of local crafts people. The 1980s also saw exhibitions, *Rag Time* at the Shipley Art Gallery in Gateshead, and *Layers of Meaning* at Woodhorn Colliery Museum, Ashington, bringing together traditional mats as well as contemporary pieces, the latter adapting the old techniques for use with modern materials.

A fresh interest in the craft brought about the formation of a number of matting groups throughout the North East, which led to the production of some exciting work by individual textile artists, using traditional methods in a modern medium. In an age where there is now an urgent need to recycle society's old waste materials, an old craft, born out of necessity, has been transformed into a new art form, which reflects the spirit of a new age; a true case of *"from rags to riches."*

Painting by North Country artist, Tom Lamb, born 1928, illustrating his mother and father in the kitchen of their pit cottage, at Blackhouse, Co. Durham, in the 1950s. Tom lived here for some 37 years, and there were always rag mats on the floor.

The painting **Geordie Ha'ad the Bairn**, of 1890, by North Country artist, Ralph Hedley, illustrates a typical miner's cottage, as it would have been at this period. Painted from life, the artist depicts a miner called Snowdon Pyle, in his cottage near Newcastle upon Tyne. The round oven, the fender made from an old wagon wheel with the spokes cut off, the fire brick floor and the clippy mat together, complete this traditional scene, which could only be in the North East of England.

Bodgy, broddy, clippy, clooty, hooky, proggy, proddy, peggy, stobby, tabby...

...all are the names for those wonderful creations we, in the north country, know as rag mats, though in other areas are recognised as rag rugs.

Pencil drawing, representing a mat-making scene of the 1930s, entitled 'Waste not want not'. The artist, Rev.Edward Lynn, born c.1914, the son of a colliery engineer, was brought up in Brandon, Co.Durham. He explains the scene, 'that is why clothes no longer in use are turned into proggy mats, that are deep and tough enough to last for ages. The whole family is involved in their making – father assembles the frame and then keeps the finished sections tense, mother "weaves", the daughters cut up old garments and roll the clippings into a ball. Meanwhile the son in law throws a scuttle of coal on the fire and hunts for his tobacco jar. The son back from school will have the honour of rolling the finished mat to declare it "open."'(54974)

THE SOCIAL BACKGROUND

THEY WERE MADE in all parts of the country, mostly by working class folk. You knew which part of the country you were in, by the name given to the rag mat! The craft demonstrates recycling at its best. Old clothes, stockings, blankets, flannel petticoats, uniforms and even the best suit, could be cut into the strips of material called clippings ready to go into the mat. The making of a rag mat was usually an all-embracing family occupation, for the long winter nights. Every member of the family took part. It was a home craft, in which men, women, and children could participate.

George Patterson, born in Low Moorsley, Co. Durham, in 1915, remembers his childhood, *'In my early days, I can remember having a bit of canvas or carpet on the floor. Me mother used to make mats. There were clippy mats and hooky mats, and there used to be always one in. We had a big set of frames, and everybody used to have to muck in. And as we got older, when we went to school, when we came home at night, all them that came from school, had to do a ball. Me mother used to roll balls up of cut old clothes, into what we called clippings. And everybody used to get a ball and what we call a progger, and when you came into the house, and you had to sit and you had to get rid of that ball, which was put into the mat before you got your tea, which was usually a bit of jam and bread or a bit of jam and dripping, but never very much, I can remember that quite well.'*

Mother's Proggy Mat

IN DAYS OF OLD, when nights were cold, around the fire we'd sit.
Some women did embroidery, others they would sit and knit.
Some made a thing of beauty great, as round the fire they sat.
And from the pile of clippings, came the famous proggy mat.
Old jumpers, trousers, socks as well, no, not a thing was bought.
God help the man who fell asleep, if she was clippings short.
A length of harn, in long wood frames, clothes pegs to hold them tight.
She'll prog and prog her clippings in, long into the night.
She'd prog and prog, with fingers sore, to get her mat complete.
"Hey Bella, where's me other sock? Ye know I've got two feet!"
Then she'd be short a bit of red, to finish off a rose.
Jack's tie would be six inches short, just how nobody knows.
Now Bella's nan turned out one night, in suit so smart and black,
A patch of lovely emerald green, showing at the back.
These makers of these proggy mats, held nothing in respect.
They'd have it done by Christmas day, no matter who they wrecked.
And all the green and blues and reds, these proggy mats were made.
If she ran short of clippings, that meant another raid.
You dare not go to bed at night, when the mats were on the go.
You dreamt of long johns wi no legs, just walking to and fro.
As you lay there in sweet repose, she darted by brown ale.
The phantom progger struck again, along the clipper trail.
No fitted carpet looked as nice, no bum so cosy sat.
As that creation made at home, a mother's proggy mat.

Arthur Davison

*(From Voices of the Trimdons tape recording,
produced by Jack Drum Arts, by kind permission
of Julie Ward, researcher)*

RICHARD MORRIS,
born 1st Feb.1895
recalled his life at Pelton Fell, Co. Durham.

'In most cases the kitchen floor was stone paved, whilst the sitting room was of wood. Since few people could afford carpets, these floors were mostly covered with clipping mats. Our kitchen floor used to take at least four to five such mats approx 2 yards and a half by a yard and a half. The mats were mostly made from discarded clothing, and if of a white colour they were dyed in various other colours and then used to form patterns. Other wool rugs were made, and often they were real works of art.'

Rag mats were made primarily for warmth but were also used for decoration in the home. They were functional as well as attractive, many of them being masterpieces of design.

Rag mats were usually made for home use. In some villages, there would be people renowned for their skills in making mats and these skilled workers sold their mats, sometimes making specials to order, featuring a family pet or best cow or horse! The making of rag mats was not only the preserve of women. The men folk were roped in to construct the large wooden frames that were used, and men also made the proggers and hooks, adapting them from keys, nails, wooden pegs and even antler. Their design skills were sometimes harnessed to draw the designs onto the hessian. In some cases, where a miner was injured or incapacitated and could not work, he would make rag mats. In one such case, in the 1950s, THOMAS WILLIAM RICHMOND of Stanhope, Co. Durham, made rag mats to fit his sitting room, staircase and upstairs, in the most imaginative designs.

JOHN HALL, *(below)* of Castleside, Co. Durham, born in 1913, was a well known mat maker in the area and produced many mats for family and friends.

These mats, were made by Thomas William Richmond of Stanhope, in the 1950s.

Thomas was largely housebound through illness, and was able to complete mats for the whole house.

A large section formed the centrepiece of the sitting room, whilst other pieces fitted into the alcoves and recesses around the room. All designs were his own distinctive creations.

The mat (left) illustrates his favourite geometric design, (1979-36) 1000 x 850mm.

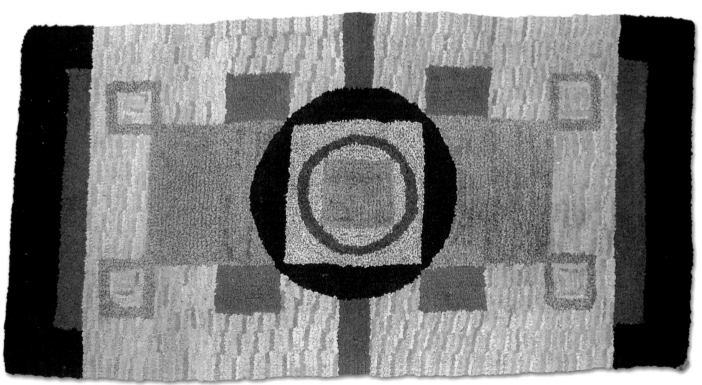

The mat (above) is very typical of a 1950s design which would not have been out of place in the Festival of Britain, (1979-36) 1360 x 680mm. There is a similarity in the design of all of his mats, essential elements being repeated in each.

Many accounts exist about the excitement and furore to complete a mat for a special occasion. To have a new mat "in situ" for Christmas or Easter was a "must" in many families and childhood memories are often associated with the smell of the new mat and the security of rolling amid the pile in front of the fire as they waited for Santa Claus. Rag mats were made and used on every conceivable occasion, for Christmas, for the "bottom drawer", for wedding presents and also at funerals!

'Our family used to make clippy mats every year in time for Christmas. The new one went on the bottom of the bed until needed'.

Ronald Dixon, Washington. (2006)

By their very nature, when worn, mats were moved from pride of place in the "best" room, or from on the bed, to the kitchen, and from there into the outside "netty", and when thoroughly worn out, were discarded, or given to the Rag and Bone man. Very few older mats survive at all.

'Women would gather to make mats – a tray of toffee would be made for them to eat whilst working. The mats were made out of old clothes and rags'.

Mrs.Spence, Hetton le Hole. (1976)

Mr.G.T.Neilson, who began work in 1934, as Public Health Inspector in Gateshead, remembers *'the hills were so steep that most of them had a hand rail on the curb, for people to pull themselves up with. Some streets were actually built in long steps. I remember going there and it was a winter's day, the roads were slippery and right down one side of the street, all of the tenants had brought out their clippy mats and laid them on the pavement. I wondered what it was for, and it stopped about half way up the street. All these mats were laid out and it turned out that there was a funeral in that house and if the streets were slippery, they put their mats out so that people could bring the coffin out and carry it down the street, and they walked on the mats to stop them slipping'.*

Friday was often cleaning day and many people remembered "dadding" the mats against the wall of the back yard or in the back street, to remove the week's grime. *'That was the main thing in the morning, shaking the mats in the street. One at one end of the mat and one at t'other shaking them up there.'*

Mrs Rutter, (born 1906)
Waterhouses, Co. Durham.

A coloured pencil sketch (above) by Rev. Edward Lynn, depicting a miner and his wife shaking the mats. c.1930. (57,016)

TOOLS AND MATERIALS

The Frame

In the North of England, rag mats were always made in a large wooden frame. In other parts of the country, people sometimes worked with the hessian on their knee, however, unless the material was held taut in a frame, it was impossible to achieve a good result.

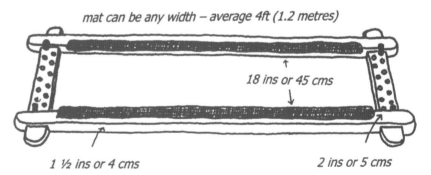

mat can be any width – average 4ft (1.2 metres)

18 ins or 45 cms

1 ½ ins or 4 cms   2 ins or 5 cms

THE FRAME was also often used for quilt making, though it was sometimes made in a smaller and more convenient size, for the making of doormats or stair carpets. It consisted of two long wooden bars or rails, up to 8ft long, with slots at each end.

Betty Lowes at Dunns Cottage, Otterburn, Northumberland making a hooky mat with the help of her next-door neighbour, c.1910. Note the trestle specially devised to hold the frame, whilst the other end is propped up on the fence. (12,043)

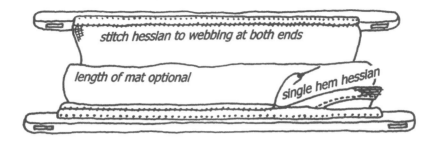

Each long rail had a piece of strong binding or webbing nailed to it. When the pattern had been marked onto the hessian, and the edges had been hemmed round, it was stitched to the webbing at each end.

Mrs ELIZABETH MARSHALL of Chopwell recalled: *'The hessian or harn, as we called it, was marked with various patterns of flowers, leaves, designs etc., cut out of brown paper, placed on the harn and chalked or pencilled around. The harn was then sewn into mat frames'.*

Only some 18 inches of hessian was left to work, the rest being wound around the other rail, nearest to the mat maker. Two flat pieces of wood, or slides in which holes were drilled to take pegs, were placed through these slots, and were held apart by pegs, holding the hessian taut. After this area had been worked, the two flat slides were removed, the finished part of the mat rolled onto the frame, the slides being replaced so that another 18 inches could be worked, and so on until the mat was completed. The use of the frame allowed fine work to be undertaken, giving an even finish, and it also enabled several people to work together at the same time.

Making mats at Consett Boys' Club, Consett, Co. Durham on 19th November 1937. (22,415)

The Materials

Once the frame had been made, the process of making a mat began with gathering the essential materials.

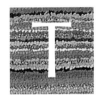 HE BASE or foundation of the mat was a piece of hessian or harn, as it was often called, which could be bought by the yard, in different widths, from the local drapery, hardware shop or from the Co-op Store. Alternatively, if you could not afford to buy the hessian, an old sack would suffice.

Mr Middlemast working in the Annfield Plain Co-op, Co. Durham, in the 1920/30s, remembered *'Those sugar sacks in the old days were made of fine harn, like a hessian, a fine hessian, and we used to sell these sacks for people who made mats, clippy mats, pulley up mats - if you take all that stitching out of that bag, you know, me mother used to do it, specially during wartime and she'd draw her own pattern on.'*

Mary Lawson, born in Houghton le Spring, Co. Durham, in 1907, recalled *'we used to get the sugar in brown sacks. We used to buy the sacks for sixpence, they used to be washed, scrubbed and unpicked and that was the back for the kitchen rugs, the clippy mats.'*

If a larger mat were to be made, two sacks would be sewn together. A number of old mats and marked hessians still retain the tell tale signs on the reverse.

'And you took your customers round behind the counter to show them the linoleums and floor coverings and hessian. There was a lot of proddy mats made. We used to sell big squares of canvas, very close woven hessian, they called it, and they sold it either by the yard without a pattern, which was in big bales you had to undo, and measure it off the length you wanted, and it was in

different widths 27,36 and 45, that was about the size of the rugs they made. And then they had squares and stamped on it was a pattern, all different patterns.' Elsie Moore, Annfield Plain Co-op, Co. Durham, 1936-37.

These mat hessians were ready marked out with a design, and were popular with those folk who could afford them. From the 1900s, in Britain, many commercially produced ready stamped hessians for mats were available, in a multitude of designs, and sizes. Many of them would seem to have been inspired by or copied from American and Canadian examples. There are probably a large number of mats that survive today, which have been made on these stamped hessians, though they may well not be recognized as commercially produced designs.

The Newcastle Quayside Market in the 1890s. There was always a good sale for second hand clothes. (37,772)

The clippings were usually old clothes of all kinds, saved over a period or gathered from kind neighbours. Woollen fabrics, blankets, tweeds, felts and red flannel petticoats were ideal, as they did not fray. Uniform jackets were particularly suitable as they were often made in bright colours and of a fine felt or Melton cloth. Tailors had a ready supply of off cuts and there were always oddments of tweed to be had from the woollen mills on the Borders. The Warwick Bridge and Otterburn Mills supplied tweeds, many of which could be spotted in an old mat! Women would queue at the mill for 14lb bags of clippings, which were sold for two shillings.

'And we used to sell clips, clippings and the clippings used to come in big bags from the Pelaw tailoring factory and I used to put them up into $^1/4$ stone packets. There was tweeds and blacks and blues.'
Mr.Pattison, West Stanley, 1924-1975.

Men's black and navy suits were favourites for the outer border. Everything from old blankets, flannel petticoats, and even old wool and nylon stockings were used.

'There was Paddy's market on a Saturday morning where they sold the old clothes,

crowds of folks went there.'

Father Stronge from Gateshead's Irish community recalled *'Now they had in the old days (1929) a thing called a clippy mat, did you hear of that - a sacred thing, and the proggy mat? They were all made of old trousers and old coats. Now that was down there. They were the carpets. They were the mats.' 'Well you used to save in the 30s, in the hard times, all your old clothes, and you used to cut the coats up – if it was decent material, you cut it into strips and if just parts of it were good, you used to cut it into small clips.'*

Expert mat makers would collect materials to be sorted into different colours, the brighter colours always being much prized and sought after. Some people even took the trouble to dye their colours to obtain special effects. From the 1930s, thrums of ready cut wool could be purchased from the carpet factories, and these were sometimes combined with wool rags in the same mat. From the 1930s, wool thrums became the material of choice, having neither the stigma of using a second hand material, nor the work involved in finding and washing the old rags.

"A Snapper-up of unconsider'd Trifles."
Winter's Tale

Tools

Different methods of making rag mats demanded different tools. Almost anything could be fashioned into a hook or a prodder.

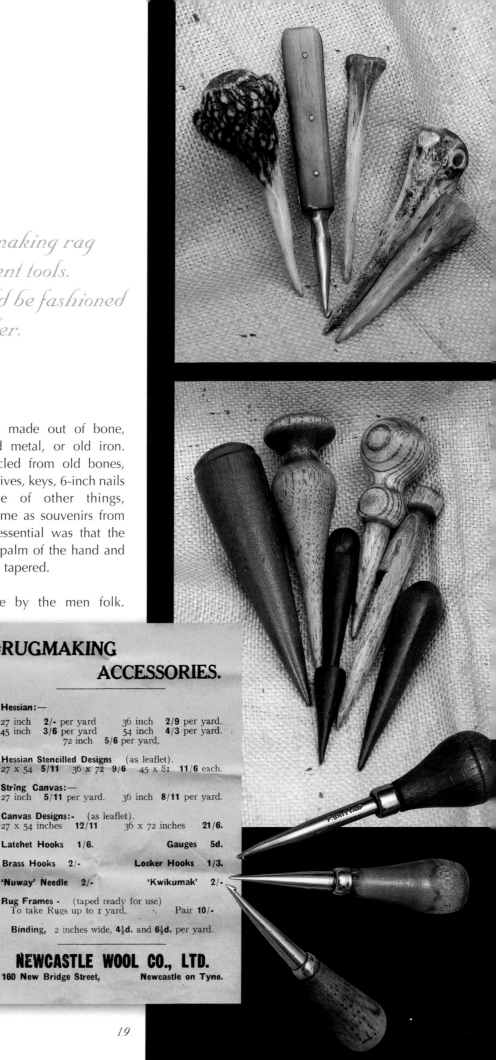

THEY COULD BE made out of bone, wood, wood and metal, or old iron. Many were recycled from old bones, pegs, tent pegs, knives, keys, 6-inch nails and a multitude of other things, including even bullets brought home as souvenirs from the First World War! The main essential was that the handle fitted comfortably into the palm of the hand and that the working end was smoothly tapered.

Many of these were homemade by the men folk. A blacksmith at Ryhope Colliery, John William Bell, born in 1882 at Hendon, Sunderland, developed a trade of making hooks and prodders. He would turn the handles, polish the steelwork, and hawk them around the mining villages. He took orders from the Co-op stores and must have made several thousand, all identifiable as they are marked RY Bell. Some hooks and prodders were made by the firm of Barlow, who also marketed the stencilled hessian designs.

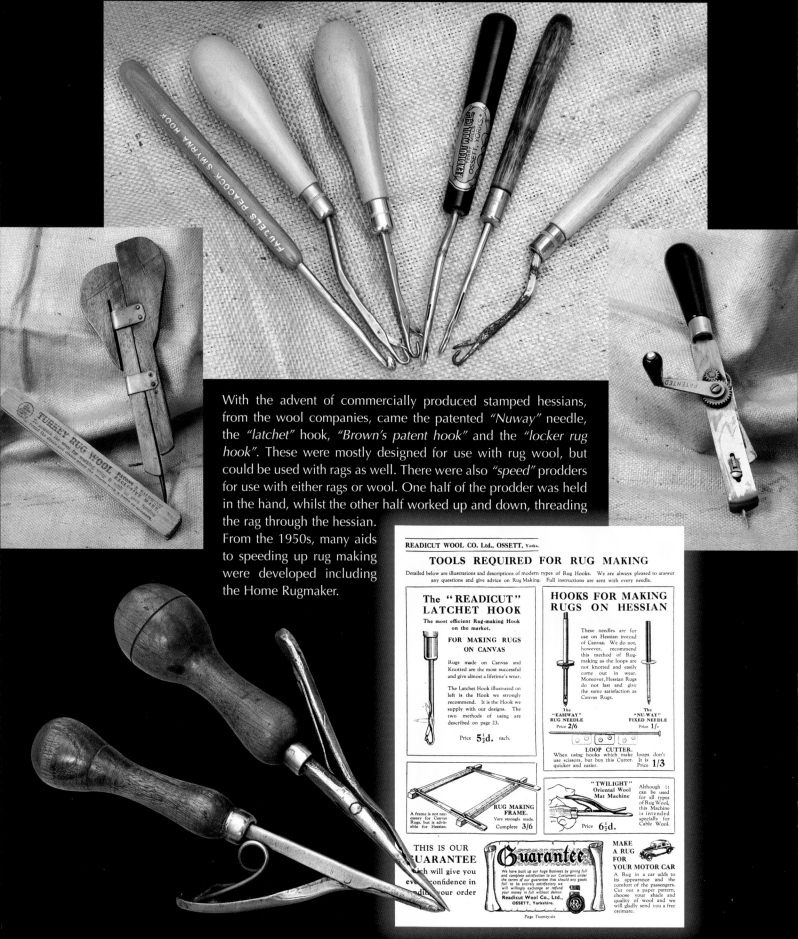

With the advent of commercially produced stamped hessians, from the wool companies, came the patented *"Nuway"* needle, the *"latchet"* hook, *"Brown's patent hook"* and the *"locker rug hook"*. These were mostly designed for use with rug wool, but could be used with rags as well. There were also *"speed"* prodders for use with either rags or wool. One half of the prodder was held in the hand, whilst the other half worked up and down, threading the rag through the hessian.

From the 1950s, many aids to speeding up rug making were developed including the Home Rugmaker.

READICUT WOOL CO. Ltd., Ossett, Yorks.

TOOLS REQUIRED FOR RUG MAKING

Detailed below are illustrations and descriptions of modern types of Rug Hooks. We are always pleased to answer any questions and give advice on Rug Making. Full instructions are sent with every needle.

The "READICUT" LATCHET HOOK

The most efficient Rug-making Hook on the market.

FOR MAKING RUGS ON CANVAS

Rugs made on Canvas and Knotted are the most successful and give almost a lifetime's wear.

The Latchet Hook illustrated on left is the Hook we strongly recommend. It is the Hook we supply with our designs. The two methods of using are described on page 23.

Price **5½d.** each.

HOOKS FOR MAKING RUGS ON HESSIAN

These needles are for use on Hessian instead of Canvas. We do not, however, recommend this method of Rug-making as the loops are not knotted and easily come out in wear. Moreover, Hessian Rugs do not last and give the same satisfaction as Canvas Rugs.

The "EASIWAY" RUG NEEDLE
Price **2/6**

The "NU-WAY" FIXED NEEDLE
Price **1/-**

LOOP CUTTER

When using hooks which make loops don't use scissors, but buy this Cutter. It is quicker and easier. Price **1/3**

A frame is not necessary for Canvas Rugs, but is advisable for Hessian.

RUG MAKING FRAME.
Very strongly made.
Complete **3/6**

"TWILIGHT" Oriental Wool Mat Machine

Price **6½d.**

Although it can be used for all types of Rug Wool, this Machine is intended specially for Cable Wool.

THIS IS OUR
GUARANTEE

...ch will give you
eve...confidence in
...di...your order

Guarantee

We have built up our huge Business by giving full and complete satisfaction to our Customers under the terms of our guarantee that should any goods fail to be entirely satisfactory we will willingly exchange or refund your money in full without demur.
Readicut Wool Co., Ltd.,
OSSETT, Yorkshire.

MAKE A RUG FOR YOUR MOTOR CAR

A Rug in a car adds to its appearance and the comfort of the passengers. Cut out a paper pattern, choose your shade and quality of wool and we will gladly send you a free estimate.

Page Twenty-six

MAKING A RAG MAT

The Proggy Mat

The proggy mat appears to be the older type of rag mat, to be made in the British Isles. This type was also made in Newfoundland and Labrador, where it was known as a "poked" mat, "prodded" or "prog" mat.

 THE MAT IS WORKED with the wrong side of the mat facing the mat maker. The rags are pushed or progged through the hessian, and the design is usually quite simple. This technique precluded the use of complicated or more elaborate designs.

This type of mat became less popular when vacuum cleaners came into use, as the suction tended to pull the clippings out. The proggy was certainly the warmest of mats, but also the heaviest and collected the dirt very easily. A good beating with a carpet beater removed the dirt but this was hard and heavy work.

1. *Cut the rags into strips approximately 1¹/₂ ins (4 cms) long and ¹/₂ to ³/₄ ins (1.5 to 2cms) wide.*
2. *With a progger poke a hole in the corner of the hessian. Using the progger push one end of a strip of material through the first hole.*
3. *Make a second hole ¹/₄ inch (1cm) to the side of the first hole and push the other end through this hole. Make sure both ends are equal.*
4. *Take another piece of material and push one end of it also through the second hole.*
5. *Make a third hole ¹/₄ inch (1 cm) further on and push the other end of the second piece of material through this third hole.*
6. *Carry on like this, running in straight lines, taking care to keep strips as close as possible as this prevents them from coming out.*

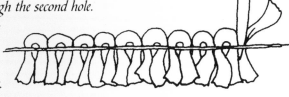

Probably the most typical design of all proggy mats, this example has outer borders in black and maroon with a hit and miss background. The mat was made by Mrs. Mary Turner of Dipton, Co. Durham in the 1960s. (2000-63.5) 700 x 530mm

The Hooky Mat

The hooky method was probably developed simultaneously in Britain and America, though the technique was perfected in America. A hooky mat is worked with the right side of the mat facing the mat maker.

THE HOOKY MAT TECHNIQUE became really popular as it lent itself to pictorial and floral designs, which could be delineated in more detail than the proggy technique would allow. The mats could be cleaned more easily and were not so heavy to shake.

1. Cut the rags into long strips ¹/₂ inch (1.5 cms) wide. If the material is thin it could be 1 inch (3cms) wide folded double.

2. Using a hook poke a hole in one corner of the hessian.

3. Holding the strip underneath the hessian, pull through the first end of the strip.

4. Poke a second hole with the hook ¹/₄ inch (1 cm) further on, and catch hold of the strip of rag underneath the hessian. Pull it through making a loop, which stands about ¹/₂ inch (1cm) to ³/₄ inch (2cms) high.

5. Continue in this way, pulling a little of the rag through the hessian, keeping the height even. When the end of the strip is reached, pull it through to the topside and trim off to the level of the loops. It is important not to leave the ends hanging underneath, as accidental pulling will remove a whole row of loops. Start the next strip as close as possible.

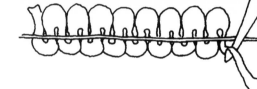

Hooky mat in stars and stripes, made by Mrs.Gibbs of Annfield Plain, Co. Durham, c. 1930s.
Born at the turn of the century, her father was a coal miner in the local mines. (1995-31) 1270 x 610mm

The Lamb's Lug Mat

Sometimes known as a dog lug mat, this type differs from the other types, as it is not pulled through the hessian. In later days the stitching was done by machine. This type of rug could be made in cotton fabric as well as in wool.

1. Cut the material into 4-inch (10cm) squares, or larger if required.

2. Fold the two opposite corners together to form a kite shape and stitch.

3. Turn inside out, creating the ear / "lug" shape and beginning at the outer edge, stitch the "lugs" in rows onto the hessian backing.

4. Continue stitching, overlapping the rows, until all the hessian is covered. The colours can be alternated by the row or varied from lug to lug.

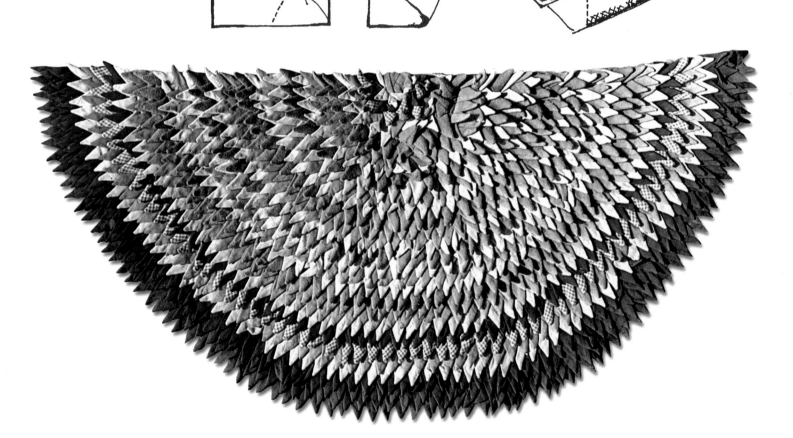

This lamb's lug mat was made by Mrs. Tom Watson of East Nettlepot Farm, Lunedale, Teesdale, probably around the 1960s. (1981-191.1) 1550 x 760mm

Braided and Coiled Mats

*Braided and coiled mats can be made from long strips of old rag,
approx. 2ins (5cms) wide and about 1 yard (1 metre) long, plaited together.*

 HE PLAITS need to be of a consistent size, varying from 1-2 ins (2.5 - 5 cms) wide, and 2/3 inch (2 cms) in thickness. The size will depend on the fabric used.

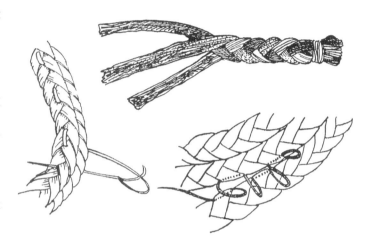

When a sufficient quantity has been plaited, the coiling can be started. With the plait lying flat, a round or oval mat can be formed. Fine string or strong cotton can be used to stitch the plaits together.

Many other types of mats were made from old rags, though these four types were certainly amongst the most popular in the North East of England.

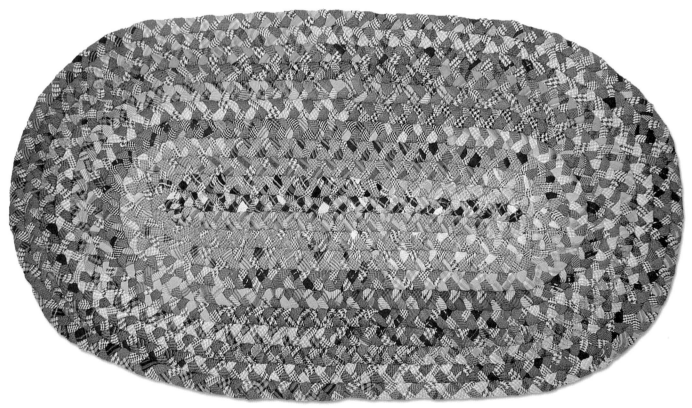

*This braided mat was made in Northumberland probably after the 1950s.
The tweed fabrics may have come from the Otterburn mill or other mills on the Borders. (1995-94) 1110 x 610mm.*

DESIGNS

Where did the wonderful designs and inspiration for the patterns come from?

ANY OF THE EARLY RAG MATS were designed and marked out, in the home, using everyday household objects as templates. It is thought that some designs were copied from the heavily carved oak furniture. Whatever was near at hand, whether it was a plate, cup and saucer, or family pet, cat or dog, these were the inspiration for many a pattern.

The design was often dictated by the amount and type of material available. Many of the older proggy mats had an outer border of black or navy material, from the husbands *"best suit"*. Black and mauve, much worn for funerals, were commonly found in borders of mats. The middle of a mat could be filled with a random "hit and miss" pattern in a mixture of colours and fabrics, the brighter colours being saved for a stylised central flower. Some mats were copied from oriental rugs, some were purely geometric, whilst others imitated crazy paving.

Templates were passed down in families from mother to daughter, and patterns could be recognised as coming from a particular mat maker.

In country areas, designs might be drawn from nature featuring trees, leaves and flowers, a favourite cow, prize bull or sheep! "Hunting Pink" from the jackets of the Hunt provided eagerly sought after scarlet. Those who lived by the sea used shells, fish and anchors for their inspiration, whilst in industrial cities, the design was more likely to be abstract, though as in the mat featuring the ship, pictorial scenes could be reproduced.

Occasionally a special commemorative mat would be made for a particular event and this might include lettering. These mats required very careful planning, and usually the husband would be brought in to help mark the hessian. Uniforms from army regiments provided colourful Melton cloth, ideal for mat making! The variety of designs was endless and the workmanship varied with the maker or makers as often every member of the family was roped in!

Unfinished hooky mat (2006-41). The pattern is obviously home designed and drawn, and may well have been done by a worker from one of the shipyards on the rivers Tyne or Wear. The black edging has probably been drawn around a plate. Clouds of black steam pour from the funnels, as the ship ploughs through the waves. 1160 x 710mm

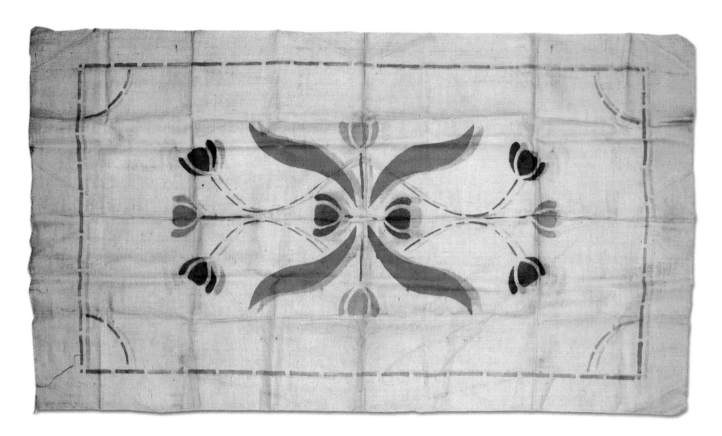

Commercially produced patterns were available in Britain from about 1900. These were stencilled onto hessian and could be bought in different designs and sizes from most drapery and Co-op stores. It is very likely that these designs were imported or copied from some of the American and Canadian patterns, which had been available in the USA since the 1850s.

In the USA, one Edward Sands Frost (1843-1894), of Biddeford, Maine, invalided out of the army at the end of the American Civil War, took to peddling and devised a method of stencilling patterns on to hessian, which he then sold ready to be worked into rag rugs. These were later printed in colour to ease the making process. Frost produced a considerable number of different designs, many of which depicted animals surrounded by wreaths of scrolls, flowers and foliage. He also produced geometric and "Turkish" designs. The firm of E.S.Frost & Co. was listed as being in business until about 1905. Huge collections of his stencils still survive in the Maine State Museum, in the USA.

Frost's ideas were later taken up by John E Garrett (1865-1937) of New Glasgow, Nova Scotia. In 1879, John Garrett first saw rug patterns on hessian (burlap) in a store window in Halifax, Nova Scotia. In 1892, he obtained a Canadian patent for his process of stamping designs onto burlap, and printed and sold his first patterns. John had started work in his father's upholstery and furniture business, but preferred to use his artistic talent in designing mats. By his third year of operation 6000 patterns had been sold.

The burlap or hessian as we call it, was made in Scotland from the fibres of the jute plant, which was imported from India. The firm of Godfrey's in Dundee supplied the material in a weave of twelve threads to the inch, to Garrett's specification. As early as 1900, he began to mail order his designs throughout Canada, the USA and Great Britain. By 1925 there were more than 100 designs, many inspired by older mats and some adapted from patterns bought in from Boston. A few have been identified as versions of Frost's designs, though most were created by John and his son Frank (1892-1958).

Garrett began his experiments with rug-hooking machines and in 1926 patented the Bluenose Rug Hooking Machine, which was sold as far afield as Great Britain. It was extremely popular, and six times as fast as a traditional hook, and although, designed to be used with rug wool, could also be used with rags. We know that, in 1924, a Mr John Kendall of Maryport in Cumberland, was Garrett's representative in the British Isles and it is likely that the Garrett designs were well known and used in the North of England. At about this time Kendall sent some samples of English rug wool to Garrett, from which he made a few small rugs for advertising purposes. They went well and the firm began production of finished rugs. These were sold in New York, helping to advertise the patterns, which became known as Bluenose Patterns.

Garrett designed several mats to commemorate the Royal visit to Canada in May/June 1939. They usually featured the rose, shamrock and thistle for the British Isles, and maple leaves for Canada. Changing times and fashions put the company out of business, their last pattern book being produced in 1974, after which time the firm closed.

Bluenose patterns, however, were bought out, and can still be purchased.

The Garrett legacy lives on. There are probably many mats, made between the 1890s and the present day still in existence, though not recognised as commercial designs. Indeed a number of stamped hessians were being sold in the British Isles, between 1920 and 1970, under the name of Barlow Design. These bear a remarkable resemblance to both Garrett and Frost patterns and must surely have been copied from them.

This 'Bluenose' design was probably produced for the British market. (2006-84) 920 x 640mm

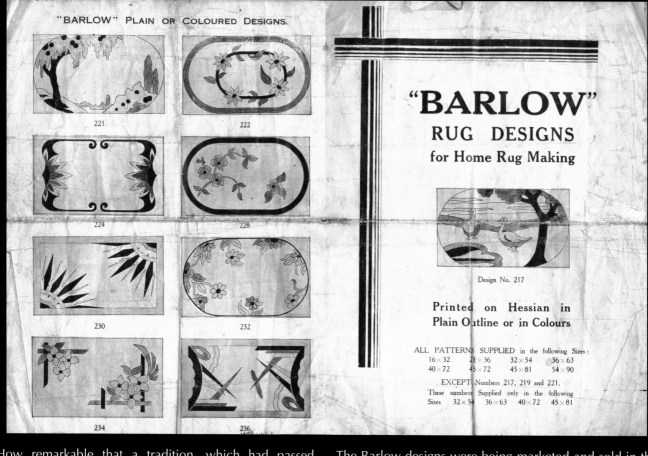

How remarkable that a tradition, which had passed originally from the British Isles to the USA and Canada, was so much influenced by the designs from 'across the pond'!

The Barlow designs were being marketed and sold in the British Isles until the 1970s, though like the Garrett designs they were adapted for use with wool, though could still be made from rags. A number of Barlow designs can be recognised in the Beamish collections.

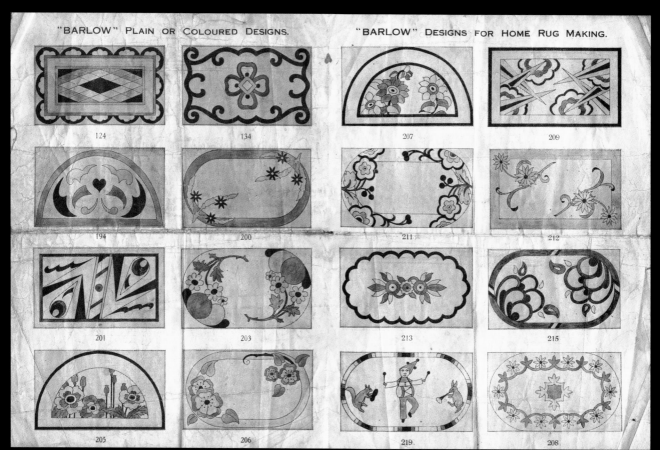

Hooky mat made by Mrs.J.Whittaker of Hobson, Co. Durham, c.1936. (1976-381) 1720 x 1110mm.

Proggy mat made by Mrs.Liza Brown of Newcastle upon Tyne, c. 1936-40. (1976-427.2) 1730 x 970mm.

These rag mats are examples of pre stamped hessians in Barlow Designs. Different methods of working the mats and the varying sizes produced very different results. Here can be seen the same designs worked using both Hooky and Proggy methods. The inventiveness of the mat maker is apparent in his or her choice of fabrics and colour scheme, which lends a unique quality to each mat. The Barlow hessians were not stamped in colour leaving more flexibility for the maker.

Hooky mat made by Mrs.Watson of Barley Mow, Birtley, c.1958. (1976-416.1) 1870 x 1120mm.

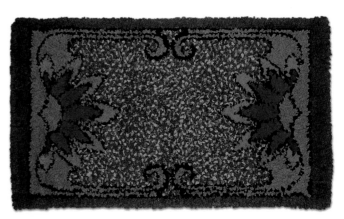

Proggy mat made by Mrs. Fairbairn of Morpeth, Northumberland, c. 1970. (1976-540.2) 1540 x 880mm.

Hooky mat made by Mrs. May Isabella Culberwell of Jarrow, c. 1945. (1985-161.6) 1750 x 1000mm.

Proggy mat made by Mrs.May Isabella Culberwell of Jarrow, c. 1945. (1985-161.8) 1750 x 1000mm.

From the 1930s to the 1960s, the making of rag mats flourished, especially throughout wartime when materials were in short supply and every old sack, rag and lisle stocking came into its own.

Gradually wool thrums from the carpet factories took the place of rags and commercial firms such as the "Readicut" Wool Company of Terry Mills at Ossett in Yorkshire marketed complete rug making kits.

The Newcastle Wool Company and the Scotch Wool Shop sold rug patterns in order to augment their sales of wool. From the 1960s, as the standard of living improved, the tradition of making mats from rags declined and there became a certain stigma attached to them.

If not worn out, many were thrown out as being thoroughly out of date, when it was possible to have a fitted carpet with so much less effort! Fortunately from the 1970s, whilst the memories of making mats were still around, there was a tremendous revival of the craft and people on both sides of the Atlantic are appreciating the skills and relearning the techniques which were so familiar in every home in the North of England.

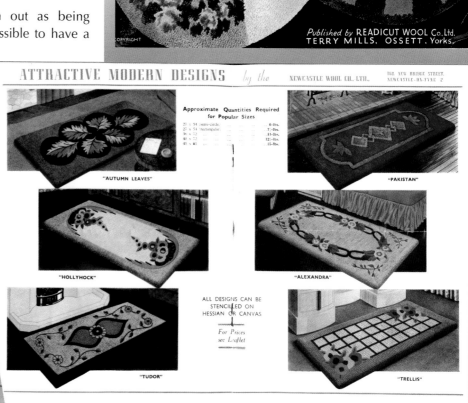

THE MATS
Stamped designs

These mats have all been worked on stamped hessians, designed for both wool and rags, as advertised in the leaflet of the Newcastle Wool Company.

ALTHOUGH THE DESIGNS date back to the 1930s, the mats were still being made up until the 1970s.

It was not unusual for mats to combine wool thrums and wool rags.

Hooky mat (top) made from wool rags. The mat maker has made the most of her rags by working them in lines to infill the background. The chain design has been lost in places. The mat was made in Blyth, Northumberland. (1983-262) 1800 x 1080mm.

Hooky mat (above centre) made from wool rags. The Newcastle Wool Company leaflet illustrates this pattern worked in wool thrums. (2005-146) 1740 x 860mm.

Hooky mat (above), made from khaki blankets and other wool fabrics. The same stamped design has given a very different result. (2005-145) 2100 x 1110mm.

Hooky mat (right) worked from grey blankets and wool rags. The red roses and bright green leaves add vibrancy to the design. (1976-313) 1470 x 910mm.

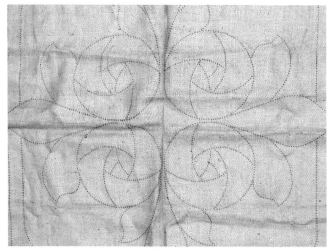

Superb example of a proggy mat made from wool rags on a Barlow stamped hessian. The design (above) owes a lot to the influence of Arts and Crafts designer Charles Rennie Mackintosh, (1868-1928). The colours are dramatic and work extremely well. A traditional black border gives definition and the background has been worked in a mixture of tweeds. (2005-139) 2020 x 1220mm.

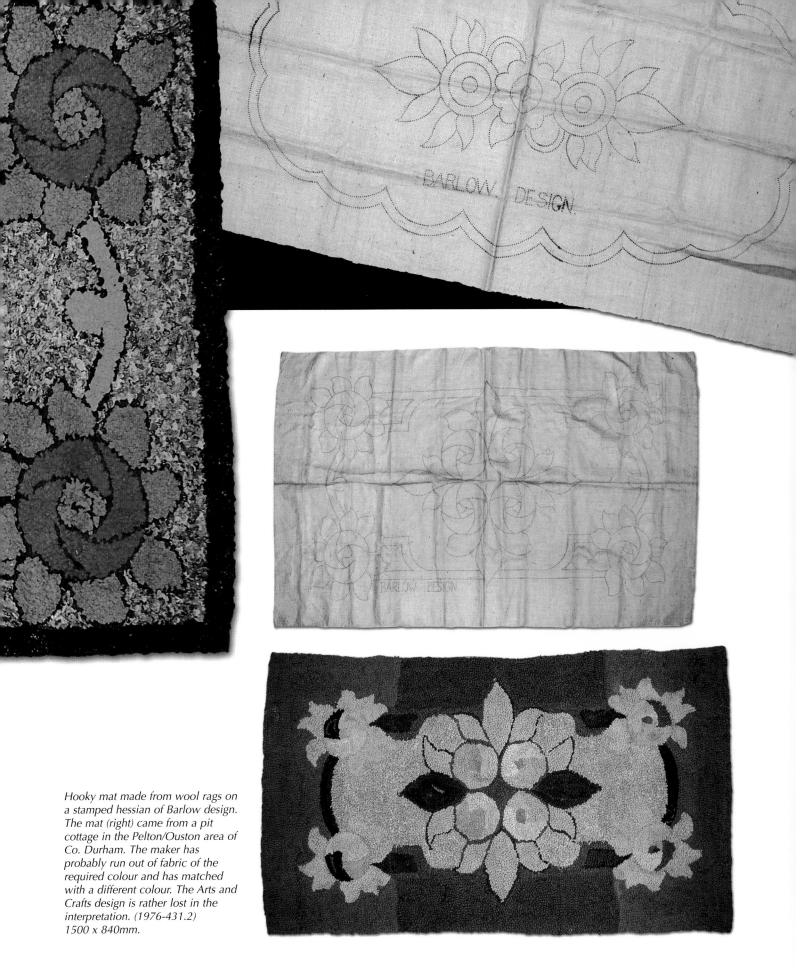

Hooky mat made from wool rags on a stamped hessian of Barlow design. The mat (right) came from a pit cottage in the Pelton/Ouston area of Co. Durham. The maker has probably run out of fabric of the required colour and has matched with a different colour. The Arts and Crafts design is rather lost in the interpretation. (1976-431.2) 1500 x 840mm.

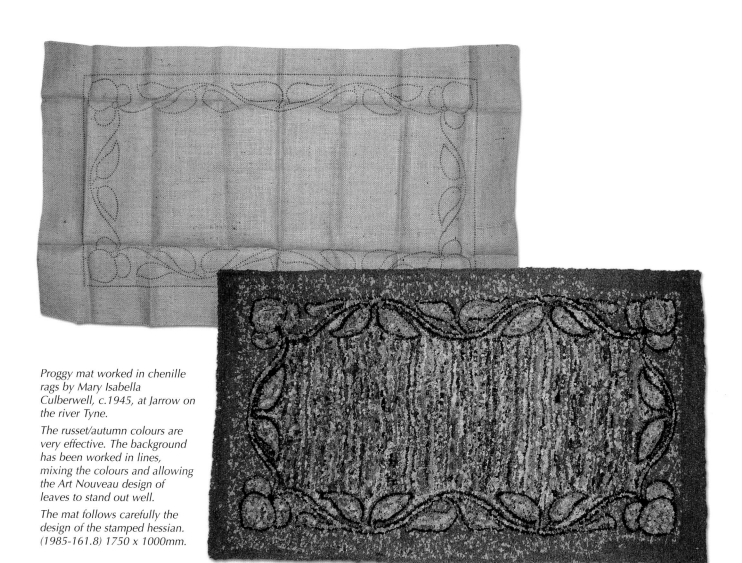

Proggy mat worked in chenille rags by Mary Isabella Culberwell, c.1945, at Jarrow on the river Tyne.

The russet/autumn colours are very effective. The background has been worked in lines, mixing the colours and allowing the Art Nouveau design of leaves to stand out well.

The mat follows carefully the design of the stamped hessian. (1985-161.8) 1750 x 1000mm.

Hooky mat made from wool rags on Barlow design hessian no.224. A number of these mats survive, worked in different materials and using different methods. The background is infilled with a lined design, blending all available colours. (2005-138) 1680 x 1160mm.

Hooky mat made from wool rags on a stamped hessian of Barlow design. The design is very typical of the 1930s/40s period. The mat was made by Mrs.Daly of Houghton le Spring, Co. Durham. The outer borders are worked in the traditional black and maroon colours, though the inner design makes a vibrant splash of colour. (1976-389.2)

1240 x 810mm.

Hooky mat made in wool rags on a stamped hessian. The design is typical of the Art Deco style and the colours reflect the period when the mat was made at Felling on Tyne c.1935. (2005-112) 1950 x 1090mm.

Hooky mat (below) made from wool rags on a stamped hessian. The design is very similar to the example on the left, though made at a much later date. It has been made in the most vibrant of colours, which would have been more readily available at the time. The mat was made by Mrs.Norma Roberts at Beamish Museum, in 1979, when the museum was beginning to develop. (1979-621.1)   1800 x 1140mm.

Hooky mat (above) made from wool rags on a stamped hessian. The pattern was often adapted by the maker to suit the design and the materials available. The colours are very tasteful and the background has been worked in lines to use up several blending colours. The mat was made by Mrs.Margaret White Colling c.1930s, of St.John's Chapel, Weardale. The mat came from a leadminer's / quarryman's cottage at Rookhope in Weardale, Co. Durham. (1976-445.1) 1480 x 880mm.

Hooky mat (below) made from wool rags on a stamped hessian. The formal design incorporates flowers linked in an oval which is filled with random hooking. (2005-118) 1240 x 780mm

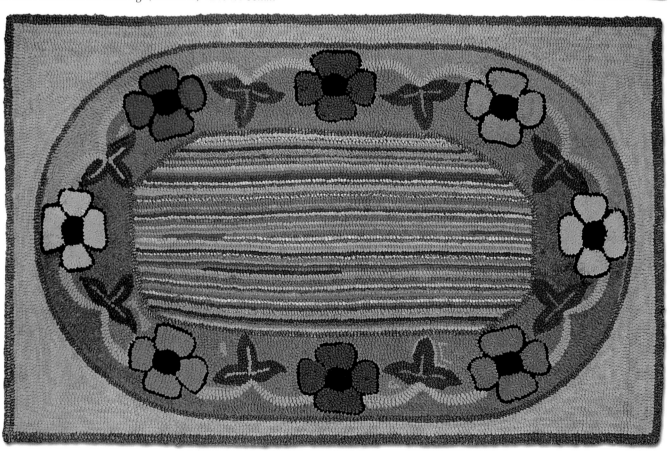

Abstracts

Proggy doormat made from wool rags. The design is the traditional "hit and miss" pattern, which took little planning and was an excellent way of using up an assortment of clippings. Abstract designs were often used in the kitchen, whilst more elaborate designs saved for the parlour.

This mat was made in Crook, Co. Durham, by one of the Cruttenden family, who worked in the local coalmines, in the early 1900s.

(1988-179.53) 770 x 580mm.

Proggy mat made from wool rags, with a very traditional border in black/navy suiting. The "hit and miss" design in the centre is brightened up by the inner border of red wool. The mat was made by Mrs.Ethel Richardson of Ashington, Northumberland, about 1960. Mrs. Richardson came from a farming family from Hirst Castle Farm.

(1976-542.1) 680 x 55mm.

Proggy doormat with black border and diamond design carefully picked out in maroon and green fabric. The mat was made in Blackhill, Co. Durham, about 1890. The family may have been employed in the local Iron Company at Consett.

(1976-449.1) 800 x 450mm.

Hooky mat made from wool rags.
The design is probably a home drawn
pattern. The hessian has been divided
into rectangles, creating a formal design
reminiscent of a garden parterre. The
rags have been cut from old blankets
and suitings, with a few bright colours
used very sparingly to add life.
(2005-141) 940 x 630mm.

Hooky mat, made from wool rags, in a
simple but formal design, which may
have been home designed, though
could also have been on a stamped
hessian. The fabrics have been saved
for the project. The mat was made in
Annfield Plain, Co. Durham. (2006-63)
1860 x 1100mm.

Hooky mat made from wool rags in a
formal design, probably home drawn.
The colour scheme is rather mute and
restricted but effective, the background
having been divided up into squares
creating a chequer board effect. The
mat was made in Tanfield Lea, Co.
Durham in the 1960s. (1979-332)

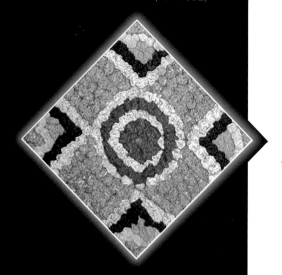

Hooky mat made from wool rags. The hessian has been very carefully marked out into squares divided into triangles, each triangle being outlined in black. The fabrics have been selected to give a good overall colour balance.
The mat was made by Mrs.Green of Stanley, Co. Durham in 1936, aged about 51 years.

(1976-797) 1290 x 890mm.

Hooky mat made from wool rags and tweeds on a Barlow hessian. An outer brown border possibly from old suiting frames an overall diamond pattern, which has been carefully designed to give a pleasing arrangement of colours, punctuated by emerald green diamonds.

(2005-119) 1680 x 930mm.

Hooky mat made from wool thrums in a similar pattern of overall squares and triangles. A great variety of colours are used with black triangles interspersed throughout.

(2005-137) 1470 x 1380mm.

Hooky mat made from wool
rags in a design of eight
octagons set on a lined
background. The colour
scheme of jade green, brown
and rose on the grey
background works well.

The mat was made by
Mrs.Craggs of Easington Lane,
Co. Durham in 1970.

(1978-927) 1730 x 1130mm.

A very large hooky mat in
multi coloured wool rags, this
has been designed with flare,
and possibly using a great
variety of household objects
for templates. The bold design
at first appears to be rather
haphazard, but it is well
balanced with circles, half
moons, twigs and hearts
spread evenly throughout.
The mat was made by Mrs
Elizabeth Ann Wilson, of East
Howl, Co. Durham, who was
born in 1913. Her husband
was a coal miner and they
had five children.

(2005-121)
2030 x 1300mm.

Hooky mat made from wool
rags. An outer border of large
squares, set on point against a
brown background with
centre is infilled with a crazy
design of lines in random
colours. The mat was made by
Mrs.Jonty Parr of Durham, a
coal miner's wife.

(1976-310) 1830 x 890mm.

Crazy designs

Hooky mat with outer grey border, and detail of squares and lines at each end. The overall crazy design is worked in swathes of green, blues and browns. The mat was made in Delves Lane, Consett, Co. Durham.

(1978-130.2) 1430 x 890mm.

This mat is an unusual combination of proggy and hooky techniques made from wool rags and tweeds. A large oval is filled with a crazy paving design in browns, blues, greens and beige fabrics, all set on a lined ground. The mat was made by Mrs.Eva Milner of Priory Farm, Muggleswick, Co. Durham in the 1940s.

(1989-65) 1960 x 1070mm.

Hooky mat made from wool rags. The design is probably home drawn and is very vibrant and colourful almost resembling a stained glass window. The crazy paving design is set into a diamond, on a lined background of brown stripes. (2005-142) 1660 x 1190mm.

Hooky mat made from wool rags. The outer borders of grey and blue were probably from old blankets. A plate may well have been used as a template for the inner border of half moons in a variety of colours. The crazy paving pattern flows across the mat in curves outlined in black, which enhances the design.
1979-134) 1240 x 980mm.

Hooky mat made from wool rags. The pattern is obviously a home drawn design, utilising typical coloured fabrics of the 1930s. The simple design of squares in each corner with a diagonal cross defines the mat, which has a background of crazy paving in jagged square shapes, outlined in black. A crazy design was an excellent way of using up all the scraps of fabric, though even here the maker has maintained a careful colour balance overall. (2000-155) 1700 x 1300mm.

Floral designs

An extremely fine hooky mat, so fine that it is difficult to believe that it has been made from wool rags, as well as wool thrums and lisle stockings! The design is relatively simple and could well have been marked using home templates. This mat was made by Mrs Annie Margaret Roddam of Steel in Hexhamshire, Northumberland. Mrs.Roddam was obviously an expert mat maker, who made some very fine mats. This mat won a prize in an Exhibition of Handicrafts in 1938. It was never used and may well have been kept for exhibition purposes.

Mrs.Roddam died in 1945 aged just 59 years.

(1980-505.2)
1260 x 710mm.

Both hooky mats, although in worn condition, are of extremely fine work. They are made from wool rags and possibly lisle stockings though the work is so fine that it is impossible to be sure about the materials. Both mats were made by Mrs.Annie Margaret Roddam of Steel in Hexhamshire, Northumberland, in the early 1900s.

The designs are highly sophisticated, the shading on each flower having been done by an expert hand. These designs bear a remarkable similarity to those being produced by John Garrett in Canada, and as Mrs. Roddam was an excellent mat maker, she may well have bought in specially marked hessians. (1980-505.4) 1330 x 760mm and (1980-505.5) 1290 x 740mm.

A very finely worked hooky mat, made from wool rags. The design is most attractive and professionally arranged, possibly on a ready marked out hessian. The colours have faded very gracefully, and though not displeasing to the eye, are dramatically different from the vibrant colours on the reverse of the mat. The mat was made by Mrs.Lattimer, (who was aged 88 years old when she died in 1959). It was a wedding present given to the mother of Mrs.Parker of Nenthead, Cumberland in 1904.

(1977-171.1) 1730 x 1100mm.

Very large hooky mat, made from wool rags, suitings and tweeds. The mat would appear to be on a stamped hessian, as the design is quite imaginative with its floral design overlapping the borders, though it does not appear to be similar to any of the Barlow patterns. The colour scheme is bright and attractive. The mat was made by Mrs. Mary Elizabeth Burn of Roddymoor Farm, Crook, Co.Durham in about 1956. (1976-459.2) 2470 x 1320mm.

A fine hooky mat (above) with stylised flower and leaf design. The black/navy border was made from old skirts and the grey background from men's shirts. The flowers and leaves stand out well on the grey lined background, which is outlined with a red border. The mat was given to Mrs.S.E. Carr of Homilton Farm at Capheaton, Northumberland as a wedding present, when she married in 1934, though it is likely according to family tradition that the mat was made in 1916 at Fourstones, near Hexham, Northumberland. (1996-115) 1570 x 735mm.

A fine hooky mat (below) not dissimilar to the example above. The black border with navy half moon shapes frames the mat, which features a flowing design of red daisies and stylised green leaves set on a lined grey background, which is in two toned pattern surrounding the leaves and flowers. An outer border of green leaves and grey and purple flowers give added interest. The mat was probably made in the early 1900s. (1994-42.3) 1520 x 840mm.

A superb example of a hooky mat made from old wool rags. The design, which is extraordinarily elaborate, seems to be a copy of a Persian rug, though we do not know if the mat was  worked on a commercially stamped hessian. Mail order catalogues of the early 1900s would have featured such Oriental style rugs and an experienced mat maker may have copied these.

This mat was made by Mrs.Laura May Baker (born 1875 and died c.1953). Mrs.Baker lived at Newbiggin by the Sea in Northumberland, and was an expert mat maker, exhibiting her mats all over and winning many competitions. A whole room in her house was set aside for mat making materials and she would dye fabrics when required. As well as being active in the Salvation Army, she took in paying guests to earn a living. She made many mats including a stair carpet, but sadly this was the only mat to survive after her death. (2005-90) 1360 x 1040mm.

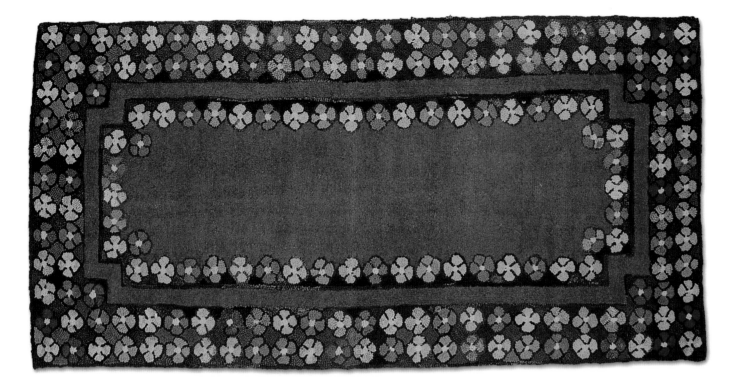

Hooky mat (above) made from a combination of wool rags and thrums, which was normal for the period when the mat was made c.1936-37. Both mats were made by a lady from Castleside, Co. Durham, and follow a similar design, which was probably her own pattern. The outer border of flowers worked from rags, adds variety to the mat, and the centre has been worked in wool thrums lending a consistency to the overall effect. The maker was skilled at making rag mats. (1980-64.1) 2200 x 1070mm.

The mat (below) combines hooky and proggy techniques. The outer border has been made from proggy thrums, whilst double rows of hooked flowers are set on a background of dark green. The centre of the mat has been hooked in lines of multi coloured fabrics, mostly in wool rags, producing a lively and pleasing result. (1980-64.2) 1790 x 1000mm.

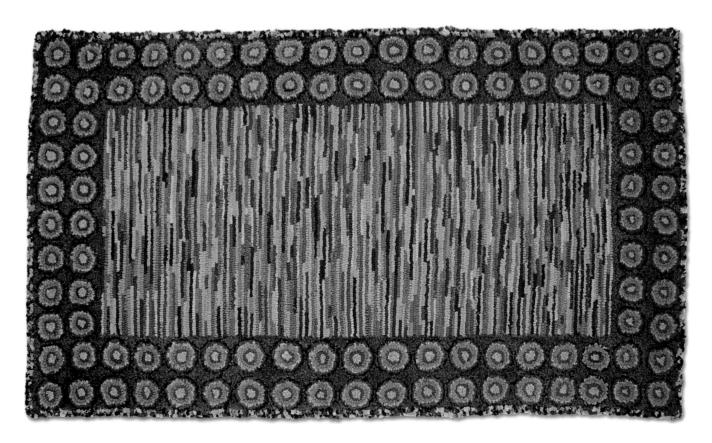

Proggy mat of wool rags and tweeds, with traditional black border and alternating inner borders of green, brown, grey and blue. The centre has what appears to be a home drawn design of leaves and flower. The mat came from High Shincliffe, Co. Durham. (1978-1029.3) 1620 x 880mm.

Very large hooky mat made from wool rags. The design is home drawn and the colours are really vivid in bright reds and greens, purple flowers, all set on a multicoloured dotted ground.

The mat (above) was made by Mrs. Mary Elizabeth Burn of Roddymoor Farm, Crook, Co. Durham about 1956. (1976-459.1) 2100 x 1340mm.

Hooky mat (right) made from mixed wool rags and thrums. The design may be home drawn and very much resembles the running feather design which a quilter would have used in the North Country. Frames were always used for mat making as well as for quilting and they were often interchangeable. The colours used for the feathers have been selected to be bright and contrasting against the lined multicoloured background. (2005-140) 1780 x 1100mm.

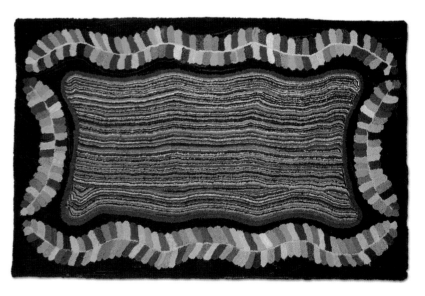

Here a fine hooky mat depicts a fox chasing game birds. The design is dramatic, the fox taking central stage. Even the lined design of the background emphasises the flight of the birds. The mat is made from wool rags and old grey blankets for the background. The mat came from the Hexham area of Northumberland and may date to the late 1800s. (1996-33) 1560 x 860mm.

Pictorial designs

Pictorial designs are not found frequently in the North other than those made by the Nicholsons and Barkers of Lanercost.

Mat making was often a male occupation and men also helped to draw the design on to the hessian.
It is likely that this mat was both made and designed by a man, who had probably been in the Royal Artillery. The motto Ubique Quo Fas Et Gloria Ducunt may be translated as Everywhere Whither Right and Glory Lead. The grey background would appear to be from an old blanket.
(2005-124)
1370 x 880mm.

This hooky mat has been worked in a combination of wool rags and wool thrums. The mat hessian may well have been commercially stamped as it is a sophisticated piece of work. Otherwise it would have been carefully copied from one of the many images of the "Crinoline Lady" that was much in vogue during the 1930s period. Teapots and tea cosies, fire screens and embroidered items all featured this design. The bright colours are well chosen, and the outlining in black of the figure adds definition. The mat came from South Shields.
(1980-391.1) 1150 x 940mm.

This wonderful hooky mat has been made from old wool rags and wool thrums. It may well be a commercially stamped hessian or if not, it has been extremely professionally designed. The "Crinoline Lady" features in a garden of flowers seen against a brick wall, and through a flower-clad pergola, a distant view into the garden beyond can be seen. The colour balance has been very well thought out and the overall effect is quite striking. (1991-11) 1990 x 1100mm.

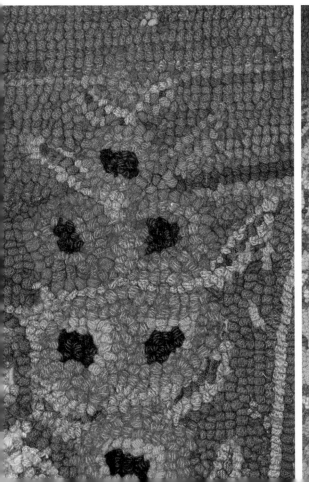

Louisa Creed took up rag mat making and specifically hooking, at the age of 50, unaware that her aunt, Winifred Nicholson, had played an important part in keeping the craft alive in Cumberland. Louisa saw an old rag mat in a museum and this prompted her to teach herself. Cats and landscapes are her favourite subjects. Louisa soon became aware that she was part of a great revival of mat making throughout the country. The importance of recycling combined with the exploration of new art forms, have inspired some really exciting work.

Such was Louisa's enthusiasm that her husband, Lewis was also "hooked", and with a great deal of enthusiasm and humour, he makes what he terms "fun rugs". Now they both enjoy sitting together in the evenings making their rag mats. A number of their mats are represented in the Beamish collections.

'Horace' made 2005 by Louisa Creed.
(2007-93.1) 910 x 1220mm

'The Seasons – Summer' made 2003 by Louisa Creed.
(2007-93.7) 810 x 860mm

'Blue Frog' made 2006 by Lewis Creed.
(2007-93.15) 700 x 820mm

OTHER DESIGNS

Lamb's Lug mats

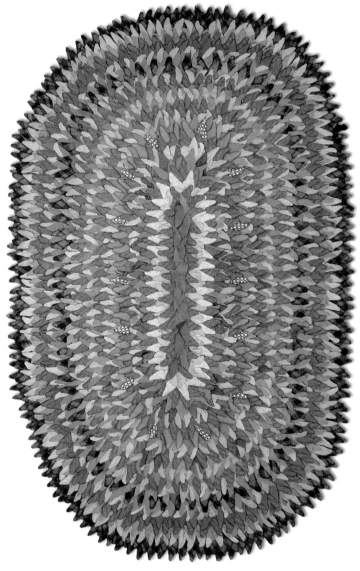

THE LAMB'S LUG, sometimes known as Dog's Lug mat was a rather more unusual type of rag mat. Instead of the material being pushed or poked through the hessian, the material was stitched onto the upper surface. This mat was made, probably around the1950/60s, by Mrs. Tom Watson, a farmer's wife, from lady's tweeds, in pale pinks, greens and mauve fabrics even including some lurex. The stitching could be done by machine, speeding up the process. (1981-191.2) 1360 x 860mm. Mrs. Watson threw nothing away. She even made net curtains out of the cotton strings from old feed sacks!

Her home at West Nettlepot Farm, Lunedale, Teesdale, was a typical northern farmhouse. Here in the kitchen her farmer husband, Tom sits by the range. A number of rag mats can be seen on the floor. (169670).

Braided Mats

Braided or plaited mat made out of old woollen tweeds. The mat came from the North East of England and was probably made sometime from the 1950s or later. The detail shows the bright fabrics in use. (1995-94) 1110 x 610mm

Braided mat made from the corduroy of old trousers, in beige and mustard.

The colours are very typical of the heavy-duty cord trousers worn by farmers, and it is likely that this mat was made and used in a Cumbrian farmhouse in the Cockermouth area. (2006-71) 1370 x 1000mm.

From Craft to Art

Heather Ritchie was born in Sunderland in 1944. Her mother and brothers had been evacuated to Reeth during the 2nd World War.

EATHER RITCHIE was born in Sunderland in 1944. Her mother and brothers had been evacuated to Reeth during the 2nd World War, and many of Heather's childhood days were spent there. Her love of the Dales led to her moving there in 1970. Heather's rug making career began, also in 1970, as a result of the move, when she needed to cover the stone flaggs of her new home, an old stone cottage in the Yorkshire Dales. A neighbour, Hanna Place, gave Heather a bag of old lisle stockings, a hook, and an old sack! Some lessons on rug making were thrown in and Heather never looked back! A rug maker called Joan Bell moved into the village and introduced Heather to new techniques of fine cutting, shading and fabric dyeing and Heather became addicted!

Her love of hooking and her skills at prodding pictorials, especially figures, and textures, have won her international acclaim. She has travelled to America, Canada, Africa and Australia, teaching and exhibiting. *'For me, the joy of rug making is in teaching the craft. I get immense pleasure from sharing the creativity, and it has given me the opportunity to make friends all over the world. I want to share this art, passing it on to future generations so it doesn't die out.'*

MODERN TEXTILE ARTISTS working in fine and applied art disciplines, and often with an art training, have turned their attention towards the craft of rag rug making. Using the old techniques, they have translated the traditional craft into a new language, based on contemporary materials and technologies. An accepted second-hand economy has presented new opportunities and an abundance of materials, which can be adapted for the craft, a complete contrast to the old days of thrift and economy! Today's rag rugs are made by choice rather than from necessity. Today's discarded waste has become the art of the future, reflecting a current need for our way of life to become more "green" and sustainable.

Contemporary artists are creating works of art, which exude colour, design and a variety of techniques. These are no longer the functional furnishings to brighten up the hearth; these are aesthetic statements, designed to be seen as wall-hangings, rather than floor coverings, in which the artist has taken the craft to a different level, interpreting a modern world.

Translating the traditional craft into a new language, these designs by Ali Rhind demonstrate how the old techniques can be integrated into modern sculpture.

ALI RHIND has developed the technique even further in her decorative interiors. Using the low-tech traditional methods of rug making, she has produced acoustic panels, seating, and also sculptural pieces, all made with recycled hand dyed wool. Born in 1954, in Wolverhampton, Ali attended Northampton School of Art, before gaining a BA in Sculpture at the University of Newcastle upon Tyne in 1976. She has since worked as community artist, furniture maker and textile artist. She has held many exhibitions of her pieces, has worked as artist in residence in hospitals, schools and libraries, and has undertaken a number of commissions. She also has time to run a number of rug making courses.

FUTURE MATTERS

It is often only when people realise that a craft is in danger of extinction, that a renewed interest is taken in it, and such was the case with rag mats.

SINCE THE 1970s, when most of the traditional makers were too old to make mats or had died, a fresh interest in recycling materials coincided with a renewed interest in the leisure craft of making rag mats. In 1970, when Beamish came into being, one of the first crafts to be demonstrated was that of making rag mats. Perhaps Beamish helped to bring mat making back into fashion!

A number of matting groups have been formed throughout the North East of England and throughout the country as a whole. The craft is now being enjoyed not only as a communal pastime, helping to relieve the stress of the modern world, but it has also become invaluable in reminiscence and occupational therapy, in many a residential home. The rebirth of the craft in the UK has paralleled that which had taken place in the USA, where a huge revival was already well established.

Woodhorn Matters group have been meeting for over 12 years, their aim being to preserve the craft by holding workshops, having exhibitions and offering outreach to a variety of community groups. They produce individual pieces and also work together on joint projects.

Further information from Sheila Wilson
email woodhornmatters@yahoo.co.uk

CLARA VALE MATTERS GROUP is a self-help group meeting at the Community Centre in Clara Vale, near Ryton. Established matters meet on a regular basis and classes for beginners can be organised. From time to time Residential Weekends are held.

Further information from Billie Turnbull,
Rift Farm, Wylam, Northumberland. NE41 8BL
01661 852127.

DURHAM CLAYPORT MATTERS GROUP aims to promote traditional and contemporary mat making in the Durham area. There is an interest in researching the history of mat making as well as in recording oral history of traditional work and learning new techniques from around the world. The Group meets at the Clayport Library in Durham.

Further information can be found at
www.durhamguild.com under Clayport Matters
Or email durhammatgroup@yahoo.co.uk

WEARHEAD MATTERS are a community group, which meets in the Village Hall at Wearhead regularly two days a week. These ladies are experienced mat makers, and they produce mats for sale and for special order. Most of the mats made are proggy.

Further information from Lyn Taylor
01388 537683

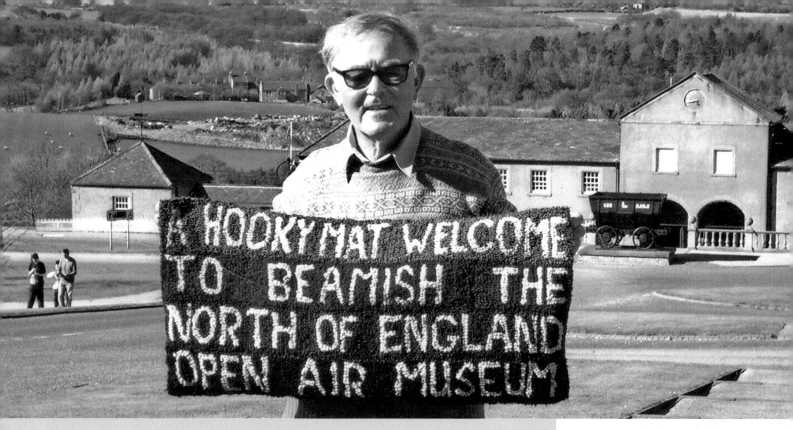

Places to Visit

American Museum in Britain,
Claverton Manor, Bath BA2 7BD

Tel.01225 460 503
www.americanmuseum.org

Beamish,
The North of England Open Air
Museum, Beamish, County Durham
DH9 0RG.

Tel. 0191 370 4000
www.beamish.org.uk and
www.beamishcollections.co.uk

Black Country Living Museum,
Tipton Road, Dudley, West Midlands
DY1 4SQ

Tel. 0121 557 9643
www.bclm.co.uk

Dove Cottage
and the Wordsworth Museum,
Town End, Grassmere, Cumbria
LA22 9SH

Tel. 01539 435544
www.wordsworth.org.uk

Museum of Lakeland Life,
Abbot Hall, Kendal, Cumbria
LA9 5AL

Tel. 01539 722464
www.lakelandmuseum.org.uk

Ryedale Folk Museum,
Hutton le Hole, North Yorkshire
YO62 6UA

Tel. 01751 417367
www.ryedalefolkmuseum.co.uk

St Fagans National Museum History,
St Fagans, Cardiff CF5 6XB

Tel.029 2057 3500
www.nmgw.ac.uk

**Sunderland Museum
and Winter Garden,**
Burdon Road, Sunderland,
Tyne and Wear, SR1 1PP

Tel. 0191 553 2323
www.twmuseums.org.uk

*Harold Spillett of Wallsend,
Newcastle upon Tyne with
the hooky mat he made
especially for Beamish in
2006. (2006-50) 870 x 410
mm. Having been evacuated
from Tyneside to Great
Salkeld in Cumberland,
during the 2nd World War,
he learnt to make mats whilst
living with his aunt, Mary
Oliphant.*

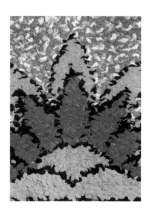

Demonstrating the making of rag mats in the Francis Street pit cottages at Beamish.

GET MATTING!

SUFFICIENTLY INSPIRED? Then start matting! There are a number of people throughout the country who can supply all the equipment needed to get started. Many also run workshops and courses and there are active matting groups in most areas.

The following supply kits, tools and materials, including hooks, prodders, hessian and frames. They also run courses.

Heather Ritchie
Shades of Heather
The Garden Studio
Greencroft, Reeth
Richmondshire
N.Yorkshire
DL11 6QT

0174 888 4435
www.rugmaker.co.uk

Ali Rhind Textiles
Ouseburn Warehouse
36 Lime Street
Newcastle upon Tyne
NE1 2PQ

0191 233 2121
www.alirhindtextiles.co.uk

Jenni Stuart-Anderson
The Birches
Middleton-on-the-Hill
Herefordshire
HR6 OHN

01568 750229
www.jenni.ragrugs.freeuk.com

Cilla Cameron Rug Maker
The Rug Studio
18 Elmcroft
Oxton
Nottingham
NG25 OSB

07752 772474
www.ragrugsuk.co.uk

Further Reading

Betterton, Sheila.
Rugs from the American Museum in Britain,
The American Museum in Britain, 1981.

Boakes, John.
Making a Rag Rug.
Smith, Settle, 2001.

Carroll, Barbara.
American Folk Art Rug Hooking,
Landauer Books, Urbandale, IA 50322, USA, 2005.

Garrad, Larch.
The Making and Use of Rag Rugs in the Isle of Man,
Folk Life, Vol.27, 1988-89.

Gilder, Diane.
Ragtime, catalogue of an exhibition at the Shipley Art Gallery, Gateshead, Tyne and Wear, 1988.

Grayson, Debra Maltzman.
Rugs and Wallhangings,
Dorling Kindersley Ltd., London, 1984.

Jeffery, G.G.
Rugs and Quilts from Shreds and Patches,
Oxford University Press, Oxford, 1942.

Kent, William Winthrop.
The Hooked Rug,
Tudor Publishing Co., New York,1937.

Kent, William Winthrop.
Rare Hooked Rugs,
Pond-Ekberg Co., Springfield, Mass., USA, 1941.

Kent, William Winthrop.
Hooked Rug Design,
Pond-Ekberg Co. Springfield, Mass., USA, 1949.

Kopp, Joel and Kate.
American Hooked and Sewn Rugs, Folk Art Underfoot,
Dutton and Co., New York, USA, 1975.

Layers of Meaning, the Rag Rug - a contemporary approach,
Exhibition catalogue, Woodhorn Colliery Museum, Ashington, 1997.

Macbeth, Ann.
The Country Woman's Rug Book,
Leicester, 1929.

Mat making,
information sheet, Beamish, The North of England Open Air Museum, 1987.

Miall, Agnes M.
Make Your Own Rugs,
The Woman's Magazine Office, London, 1938.

Proggies and Hookies,
leaflet,
Beamish, The North of England Open Air Museum.

Shepherd, Gene ed.,
The Rug Hookers' Bible,
J. Richard Noel, Lemoyne, PA 17043-1420, USA, 2005.

Stuart-Anderson, Jenni,
Rag Rug Making,
Traplet Publications, Upton upon Severn, 2003.

Tennant, Emma.
Rag Rugs of England and America,
Walker Books, London, 1992.

Acknowledgements

I would like to thank the many people throughout the North of England, who have donated rag mats for the Beamish Collections; without them this book could not have been written. Back in 1970, when I was appointed to the first post at Beamish, a plentiful supply of rag mats could be found, usually waiting for the bin man to collect! Nobody wanted rag mats in their houses in those days, as they were associated with a harsh working life. However, now, they are deservedly recognised as pieces of Folk Art, truly the fabric of people's lives; so much hard work, enthusiasm and energy have created them, and many a mat could tell its own story. These works of art will take their place amongst the other wonderful treasures at Beamish, which have been saved for future generations to appreciate.

Not only have I had the wonderful opportunity of collecting these rag mats, but I have also been able to observe a past generation, brought up in the tradition of producing them. At Beamish, we have been able to show our visitors some of the old techniques of making mats and our demonstrators, too many to mention here, have done a sterling job over the last thirty years, in continuing to make them.

Thanks must go to Rose Lewis, and Denise Hodge who trained many of our younger staff, to continue the tradition. A special thanks must go to Ann Huntley, whose liveliness and great enthusiasm, together with her gallant band of volunteers, has led to exhibitions of rag mats encouraging many people to join local groups and keep the craft alive.

Rag mats are not the easiest objects in the world to photograph and Justin Battong, Paul Castrey and Julian Harrop have risen to the challenge, producing some excellent photographs. Thanks for their patience in what appeared to be a never-ending task. Thanks also to Duncan Davis for the photo of East Nettlepot Farm, David Lawson for the photos of Ali Rhind, and to Shirley Slater for the Woodhorn photo. Once again Ian Brown has excelled. His design has produced a superb publication, which will surely inspire future matters.

Especial thanks must go to John Gall, who, as past Deputy Director of Beamish, has always given me great encouragement. His knowledge and appreciation of north eastern material culture and traditions is second to none!

Beamish is most grateful to Renaissance North East, the Regional Museums Hub, who have grant aided the origination of this book, making its publication possible. Most of all thanks must go to the Beamish Joint Committee and authorities at Beamish who have funded the publication.

RENAISSANCE NORTH EAST
museums for changing lives

MUSEUMS LIBRARIES ARCHIVES
NORTH EAST